Grace
Pre-School

GRACE COOPERATIVE
PRE-SCHOOL
2100 TICE VALLEY BLVD.
WALNUT CREEK, CA 94595

THE ART OF LEARNING
THROUGH MOVEMENT

THE ART OF LEARNING THROUGH MOVEMENT

BY ANNE AND PAUL BARLIN / *Barlin Method of Instruction*

PHOTOGRAPHS BY DAVID ALEXANDER

A Teachers' Manual of Movement
for Students of All Ages

from the Film, Learning Through Movement

THE WARD RITCHIE PRESS

DEDICATION

To all the children who participated in the classes over the many years,
helping to create the stories and fantasies.

And to those children who have become the new, young teachers,
Cappy Israel, Tamara Greenberg, Karen Kenmir, Leanne Mennin,
Martha Miyazawa *and* Shirley Thompson.

Additional photographs on pages 31, 74, 75
courtesy of Ossie Scott.

INSTRUCTIONAL SERIES BY ANNE AND PAUL BARLIN
Dance-A-Stories, books-and-records published by RCA and Ginn & Co.;
Little Duck, Balloons, Noah's Ark, Magic Mountain, Flappy and Floppy,
Brave Hunter, The Toy Tree, At The Beach.

FILM, Learning Through Movement
      Distributor, S-L Film Production
           5126 Hartwick St.
           LA., Cal. 90045
           213-254-8504

INTRODUCTION

I called the Barlins after reading about half of the book. Anne answered. Did they want me to note typographical errors? There were some *is*es that should have been *as*es and *it*s.

". . . and on page 11 the reader is instructed to spank his buttocks with his toes, but you show the model spanking his buttocks with his heels. I guess you meant to says 'heels' "?

"No, I *don't* mean heels. If they think of spanking with their heels they will miss the extended feeling of trying to hit their bottoms with their toes. Of course, they won't be able to make it with their toes, but that's not important. I want them to get the feeling of spanking with their toes because it will help them move their legs way out and backwards. Spanking with the heels can be done by moving the legs straight up which is not what we want."

I tried it. As always, she was right-on. Try it.

You can't get to the same place the Barlins get to if you rely on logic or only think in end-product terms. It is their keen insight into processes that create the opportunities for a wide range of kinesthetic experiences that is so uniquely characteristic and so "Barlinesque."

Through the development of situations and fantasies, purposes and goals are kept subtle and failure is impossible. Above all, the student is drawn into the experiences in a total, unselfconscious way. By suggestion and analogy he moves outside himself while becoming aware of his own internal experiences.

LEWIS ELLENHORN
Associate Professor of Psychology
Pitzer College, Claremont, California

PREFACE

Children WANT to learn. The key is TOTAL INVOLVEMENT

When a child has put all of himself into an experience—his body, his

mind, his emotions, his imagination and his enthusiasm—he will learn

and he will grow. He will grow not only in the specific experience at

hand, but through his entire personality.

NOTE: *A series of dots is used in the text to denote passage of time,*
     to allow students to react or to complete a movement.

ACKNOWLEDGEMENT

We would like to thank the artists and teachers whose Art concepts and
teaching techniques in Dance, Drama, Music and the Visual Arts
have been a strong influence in the growth and development of this
material:

Constantin Stanislavski, Emile Jacques Dalcroze, Kimon Nicolaides,
Doris Humphrey, Charles Weidman, Lester Horton, Trudi Schoop *and*
Benjamin Zemach.

THE AUTHORS

CONTENTS

Involve your children through
STORIES

Listening to stories is a child's way of learning

I

BEACH BALL (WALK)

STORY:

"One day, you're at the beach playing with a beach ball. It's a very windy day and the ball keeps flying over your head and out into the ocean. You're getting wetter and wetter, and colder and colder, until finally you get very angry. You say, 'Now look here, you naughty beach ball, I'm going to give you a spanking!'

"You hold the Beach Ball very firmly with both arms (so it can't fly away) and you spank it with each knee as you walk."

EXPLAINING THE MOVEMENT:

Hold your arms round in front of you, as if you're holding a large beach ball. Each time you step, bring your knee high to touch the ball. Hit the ball with one knee, then the other. Take a step — with — each — beat — of the music — step — step — step — step — Touch — the — beach — ball — Keep — your — back — up — high . . ."

HINT:

If the student cannot feel the beat, walk beside him saying, "Touch — touch," or "Spank — spank," while you too are doing the movement. If he continues to have difficulty, ask him to say the words with you. The rhythmic sound of his voice supports the natural rhythmic feelings in his body.

ACCOMPANIMENT: Side I, Band 1 or . . .

Provide your own accompaniment with drum or hand claps. Play a deliberate march tempo, slow enough to allow the student to raise the knee high with each step.

(Be sure that your students have accomplished *Beach Ball* well, before going on to the *spanking* rhythm.)

WALKING RHYTHM:

Walk _____ _____ _____ _____

SPANKING

(RUN)

Smile . . .
Smile with your whole face
Pretty soon your whole body will be smiling.

STORY: (to younger students)

"Have you ever done something you know you weren't supposed to do? Has anyone ever said he would spank you? Well, if anyone ever does say he will spank you, you can say to him, 'You don't have to spank me, I've learned how to spank myself, with my feet! Look!' "

EXPLAINING THE MOVEMENT:

"Open your arms wide and run, bringing each — foot — high — up — in — the — back. You are *spanking* yourself with your toes."

ACCOMPANIMENT: Side I, Band 2

If you prefer your own accompaniment, instead of using the record, use a drum or handclaps. The beat is exactly half as long as *Beach Ball*.

COMPARATIVE RHYTHMIC BEATS:

Walk _____ _____ _____ _____

Run ____ ____ ____ ____ ____ ____ ____ ____

DEVELOPMENT A:

The students move in a circle, alternating WALKING and RUNNING, in response to the unexpected changes of rhythm.

DEVELOPMENT B:

Teacher, call the class together as though to share a secret, "This time we're going to fool the music. When the music plays WALKING, we will *run*. When the music plays RUNNING, we will *walk*."

11

GIANT STEPS (LUNGE)

STORY: (for younger students)

"Once there was a big flood. The water went higher and higher. The houses broke loose from their foundations and floated on the water. The kittens and the puppies and the children inside the houses were very frightened.

"They didn't have to be frightened because nearby lived a friendly giant, who picked up the houses one by one and saved them from the flood."

EXPLANATION OF MOVEMENT: (younger students)

"Imagine you are the giant. Pick up a house and put it carefully on your head. Hold your back up straight, so you can balance it. Now, take g-r-e-a-t, b-i-g giant steps. Push hard with your legs because the water is heavy."

EXPLANATION: (for older students)

Note: Use the word "lunge" instead of "giant step."

"Take a long, low step forward . . . Your front knee is bent very low. Your other leg is stretched long and straight behind you. Your back is up straight as if you're balancing something on your head. This is a *lunge.*"

ACCOMPANIMENT: Side I, Band 3

If you do your own accompaniment, beat a gong for this long, slow rhythm.

DEVELOPMENT:

Ask the students to do the *lunge* while you play the *walking* rhythm.

(Two WALK beats for each LUNGE step)

Then reverse it; ask the students to WALK while you play the *lunge* rhythm.

COMPARATIVE RHYTHMIC BEATS:

Walk   _____ _____ _____ _____

Run   __ __ __ __ __ __ __ __ __ __ __ __

Lunge   _____ _____

13

SATELLITES

STORY:

"You are a satellite in space. Your feet and fingers are sending out very fast signals. Hear each beat of the music as you tap-tap-tap-tap. Come up on your toes. You make a better sound that way. Turn slowly as you tap. If you get dizzy, turn the other way."

ACCOMPANIMENT: Side I, Band 4

The beat of *Satellites* is exactly one-fourth as long as the (basic) WALK-ING beat. (The tempo on the record is a bit faster than the 4-1 ratio, in order not to dampen the spirit of the music.)

HINTS:

If the students make the "beep" sound—in imitation of the real satellites, encourage them, as part of using their voices with their movements. It makes for more complete involvement.

Percussion instruments may be played by some of the students to accompany the dancers. Such instruments might include finger cymbals or small rhythm sticks to simulate the "signals."

COMPARATIVE RHYTHMIC BEATS:

Walk	_____	_____	_____	_____
Run	__ __ __ __	__ __ __ __
Lunge	_____	_____
Satellites	- - - -	- - - -	- - - -	- - - -	- - - -	- - - -	- - - -	- - - -

When the students have experienced in dance movement, the relationship of the four rhythms, standard musical notation of these rhythms will make sense to them.

14

CORNER GAME

PREPARATION:

The *Corner Game* is a cumulative game, made up of the four previous ones: WALK, RUN, LUNGE, SATELLITES. Be sure the children have practiced all four well before playing this one.

Each of the four groups of children, *walkers, runners, Giant-steppers,* and *satellites,* begins in a different corner of the rhythms area. It doesn't matter how many students there are in each group.

EXPLANATION TO STUDENTS:

"I'm going to play each of the rhythms, one at a time. When you hear your rhythm, come out of the corner, doing your movement. Everyone stay with your group.

"When you hear the rhythm change, sit down immediately and listen for your rhythm to come again. Only one group moves at a time."

Make it a matter of group pride that the entire group responds promptly.

ACCOMPANIMENT: Side I, Band 5

When doing your own accompaniment (drum), always start with the *Beach Ball* (Walking), so that the basic beat is established, both for you and the students. Once the game is underway, however, vary the sequence of the rhythms so that the students do not anticipate their turn and lose the listening value of the exercise.

HINT:

Designate each of the four rhythms to a separate corner of the rhythms area. Rotate the groups when you repeat the game, so that each student can experience each of the four rhythms.

15

When you motivate a child you touch his inner spirit and kindle his desire to move.

an image . . .

a story . . .

M O T I V A T I N G

. . . a feeling in your voice

can motivate.

Tell the self-conscious 12 year old girl that she is "a beautiful Tahitian maiden, walking to a joyful festival carrying a basket of flowers on her head."

Tell the undersized 6 year old boy that he is "a great giant, lifting and carrying a whole house on his head."

Be A N G R Y when motivating them for the "slashing of the swords."

Be caught up in the A W E and wonderment of "making a magic."

Be as rollickingly C O M I C as the students when the "bear is trying to escape the bees."

Involvement through

FANTASY

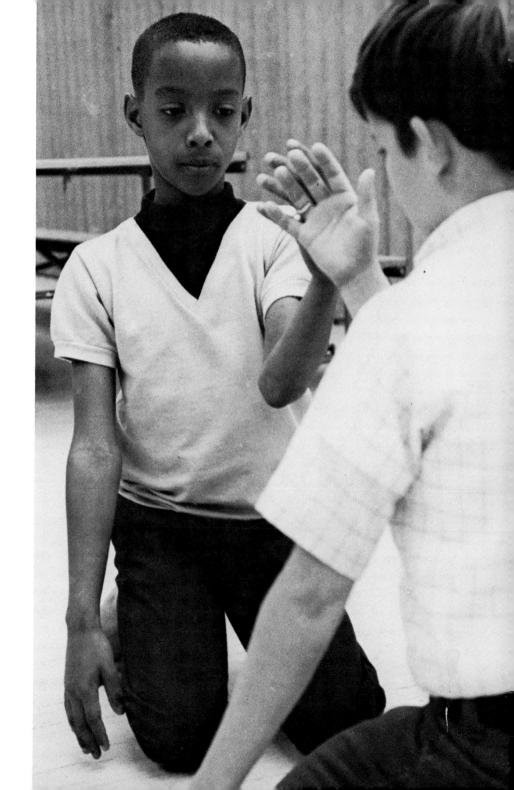

A CHILD USES FANTASY

to explore new experiences

to stretch his imagination

to keep alive his curiosity

to exercise his creativity

MIRROR REFLECTIONS

FANTASY:

(Teacher demonstrates with a partner. Face each other.)

". . . I am looking into a mirror . . . Bill is my reflection . . . I move my arms so sl — ow — ly, that Bill can mo — ove ex — act — ly with me . . . just like a mirror reflection. . . . I can see my partner moving . . . with . . . me . . .

". . . Let's all try it. Get partners. . . ."

EXPLANATION TO STUDENTS:

"With your partner, decide who is the one standing in front of the mirror, the initiator. The other person is the 'reflection'. The initiator improvises the movement, keeping . . . it . . . very simple . . . and mo — ving . . . very . . . slowly. . . ."

HINT:

Move around the room quietly as the students work. Whisper instructions to the individual leader who is rushing ahead of his partner, "Wait for your partner . . . stay with him. . . ." Slow the leader down with your quiet, encouraging voice until you feel that he understands.

18

MIRROR REFLECTIONS

ACCOMPANIMENT: Side II, Band 1 or . . .

Silence is best for this. It allows for the closest, most sensitive communication.

NOTE:

This exercise is really successful only when two people achieve the "magic" of being locked in deep movement concentration with each other. To this end, the leader moves very slowly and only as he senses that his partner is with him.

ADAPTATION*

Give each student two scarves of different colors—one for each hand. Partners are to have matching colors, so that when facing each other, the blue scarf is reflecting a blue scarf, yellow one, a yellow one. This bit of visual structure helps the students feel more secure.

HINT:

If you have had some difficulty in relating to a particular child, or he with you, partner with him in this exercise and see if something new and positive happens between you.

Suggested by TMR teacher, Kate Olsen.

PREHISTORIC ANIMAL

FANTASY:

"You are a prehistoric animal, walking on all fours. You weigh about 5,000 pounds."

EXPLANATION OF MOVEMENT:

"Reach your hands to the floor. Fall forward, putting your weight onto your hands, keep your heels down and walk—walk—walk—walk, to the beat of the music."

DEVELOPMENT A:

Establish a more disciplined order of hands and feet by saying, "hand—hand—foot—foot."

RHYTHM

hand	hand	foot	foot
1	2	3	4

DEVELOPMENT B:

FANTASY:

"You're an *adolescent* prehistoric animal. (You weigh only 500 pounds.) You don't want to walk slowly like your parents."

EXPLANATION OF MOVEMENT:

On the words, "hand—hand," advance each hand in turn. On the words, "jump—jump—jump," with feet together, jump to one side, then to the other, then forward.

ACCOMPANIMENT: Side II, Band 2

RHYTHM

hand	hand	jump	jump	jump
1	2	3	&	4

PURPOSE OF TECHNIQUE:

Stretch Achilles Tendon and Calf and Hamstring muscles. Excellent warm-up for jump type techniques.

FANTASY:

"You're the strongest man in the world. Imagine that you're squeezed between two pianos."

EXPLANATION OF MOVEMENT:

"Put one hand against each piano and pu — ush. . . . The pianos are heavy . . . It's ha — ard wo — rk . . . But slo — owly . . . they begin . . . to mo — ove apart. . . ."

TEACHER, CHECK THESE:

Feet should be apart and well-planted on the floor.

Correct the tendency to lift the shoulders by suggesting, "Joe, drop your shoulders. Make your neck long."

Watch for "swaybacks." Hips should be directly under the shoulders with stomach pulled up.

PURPOSE OF TECHNIQUE:

To strengthen the arms and shoulder muscles.

PIANO PUSHERS

ELEPHANT TAKING A SHOWER

FANTASY:

"You're an elephant taking a shower."

EXPLANATION OF MOVEMENT:

"Stand with your legs apart. Your knees are straight.
Bend forward, dropping your head and arms toward the floor.

"Clasp your hands together and stretch your arms long, like an elephant's trunk. Keep your head down, so that your arms stay close to your ears.

"When the music starts, bob down toward the floor, as though you are scooping up water in your trunk. Then swing the trunk upward, raising your shoulders only as high as your hips. Your back, arms, and head are now parallel to the floor. Reach your arms over your head as though you are trying to *shower* your back. At the same time, keep your back from coming any higher, so that you get a good stretch.

"All of this takes place in three beats. On the next three beats you drop down and rest, in the original position."

ACCOMPANIMENT: Side II, Band 3

drop	lift	lift	drop	rest	rest
1	2	3	1	2	3

HINT:

Try to lift the arms above the ears.

PURPOSE OF TECHNIQUE:

To make the back strong and flexible.

The beginnings of a self-disciplined work attitude can be found in their willingness to apply themselves to these difficult techniques.

23

JACK-KNIFE

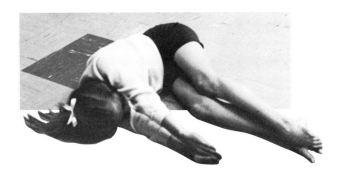

FANTASY:

"You are a champion diver practicing for a perfect jack-knife."

EXPLANATION OF MOVEMENT:

"Lie on the floor on your side, stretched out long . . . Your arms are reaching out over your head . . . You are looking up at your fingers.

"With your knees straight, stretch your hands and feet behind you, arching your body backward like a bow.

"Now, still keeping your knees straight, jack-knife your body forward so that your arms and legs come together in front of you.

Repeat:
      Arch . . . and jack-knife. Arch . . . and jack-knife. Now try it on the other side."

HINT:

Stretching the toes is an important part of this exercise. However, don't say, "Point your toes." Say something like, "Stretch your toes to get the long, beautiful curve of the diver."

ACCOMPANIMENT: Side II, Band 4

PURPOSE OF TECHNIQUE:
To make the back flexible; to strengthen the abdomen muscles.

SITTING JACK-KNIFE or "THE CRADLE"

FANTASY: (ages 7 and up)

"Now you're a jack-knife in a sitting position."

THE CRADLE
FANTASY: (ages 4 to 7)

"Let's make a cradle. Put a baby in your lap. . . .
Now, let's rock him to sleep."

EXPLANATION OF MOVEMENT:

"Sit up. Bend your knees toward your chest.
Reach your hands toward your feet. Your toes
are as high as your knees. . . . Rock gently from
side to side . . . First on one hip . . . Then onto
the other . . . Keep rocking . . . Your stomach
and back muscles are holding you up."

ACCOMPANIMENT: Side II, Band 3

HINT:

Get involved with each child's fantasy. Offer
each a pretend stuffed animal to put in his
cradle.

PURPOSE OF TECHNIQUE:

To strengthen the abdomen muscles.

25

Involve your children through

VIGOROUS
MOVEMENT

VIGOROUS MOVEMENT

is a child's way of releasing his energy, his tensions—freeing him to relax, absorb and learn

JUMPS

FANTASY: (for younger students)

"You are a pogo stick with rubber tips on the bottom of your feet. Put some springs in your ankles and knees and bounce . . . bounce . . . bounce."

(for older students)

"Imagine you are springing on a trampoline or a diving board. Instead of landing when you hit, you bounce right up again. Keep bouncing, bouncing, bouncing."

EXPLANATION:

"Put your feet together and jump your way to the opposite corner of the room. Let the arms hang down as you jump, and straighten your backs . . . jump . . . jump . . . jump. In the air your legs are long (pogo sticks don't bend), streamline the body. When you land, bend the knees so you can push off again.—jump . . . jump . . . jump."

ACCOMPANIMENT: Side III, Band 1

PURPOSE OF TECHNIQUE:

To strengthen the hip and leg muscles.

28

A slide moves laterally across the room. If you demonstrate the movement, most of the children will be able to repeat it from your demonstration.

SLIDES

EXPLANATION:

"Open your arms wide. Face me (front) and slide across the room, one at a time. Look into my eyes as you pass.

Now let's slide back the other way, still facing me."

TEACHER:

By having the child facing front while sliding in both directions he will find it necessary to give each leg a turn to lead out. This gives you an opportunity to detect a possible laterality problem. If the child is having difficulty with it, break it down for him with, "Step to the side and *hear* the other foot sliding to it. If you slide the foot, you can hear it because it makes a sliding sound on the floor."

This simple motor skill, the slide, done repeatedly, can help to correct a laterality problem.

PURPOSE OF TECHNIQUE:
To develop confidence in the use of each leg.

HINT:

If a child needs your individual attention, take his hands in yours, ask him to look into your eyes, and slide in both directions with him.

ACCOMPANIMENT: Side IV, Band 1

Giving a child confidence in the use of his body restores the instinctual joy of movement.

LEAPS

DEFINITION:

A "leap" is a change of weight—in the air—from one leg to the other.

STORY: (for young students)

"You are a huge bird flying high in the sky. Imagine that the shoe in the middle of the room is a very high mountain. With your "wings" (arms) wide, you run fast, as though flying, until you get to the "mountain." Then take a big leap, stretching your legs long (one in front, the other in back) . . . and over you go!"

EXPLANATION:

Everyone line up in one corner of the room. One at a time, run as fast as you can across the room . . . and leap over the shoe . . . Stretch your legs as wide as possible and soar as high as you can.

HINT:

They may persist in using their arms as though running for track. In that case, say, "open your wings, like a plane or a huge bird so you can soar through space."

PURPOSE OF TECHNIQUE:

To develop strength and stretch of the legs.

DEVELOPMENT:

Place two "mountains" (shoes) on the imaginary diagonal line, spaced carefully so that the students can do one leap after the other, using alternate legs. They take no steps in between. As they learn to stretch and "give each leg a turn," challenge them further by gradually widening the space between the shoes.

HINT:

For the child who is having difficulty with this, lead him by the hand to the "mountain." Holding his hand and doing the movement with him, ask him to take a big, giant step over the first shoe and then another, with the other leg, over the second shoe. "Walking it through" once or twice helps reduce the fear of using the "weaker leg." Praise his effort. Then, holding his hand, run with him a little way, giving him a slight boost with the pressure of your hand as he takes the two leaps.

THE WEAKER LEG:

Most children will naturally leap on their stronger leg. It takes a great deal of courage to lead out and land on the "weaker leg." Many of the children have developed this courage through early games, but many have not. Be patient and kind, but persistent. The earlier they can overcome this fear, the happier they will be with themselves. The problem often clears itself up, magically, when you put down three "mountains" and ask for three successive leaps. Suddenly the "weaker leg" takes courage.

ACCOMPANIMENT: Side III, Band 2

The music provides background excitement, but use the drum accents for the leaps. It gives individual attention to each student.

Use a "roll" on the drum for the length of the "run," then a strong accent just before the student hits the air for the leap, as though you were picking him up with the beat.

For the two leaps, the accents come immediately after each other.

WHEN YOUR CHILDREN DANCE

they adjust to each other's movement

      they adjust to each other's rhythms

they become sensitively aware of each other

      they relax with each other

    they create together

      they feel free together

they communicate with each other

they learn from each other

      they enjoy each other

THROUGH MOVEMENT THEY ARE RELATING TO EACH OTHER

directly

    simply

        joyfully

           and HONESTLY

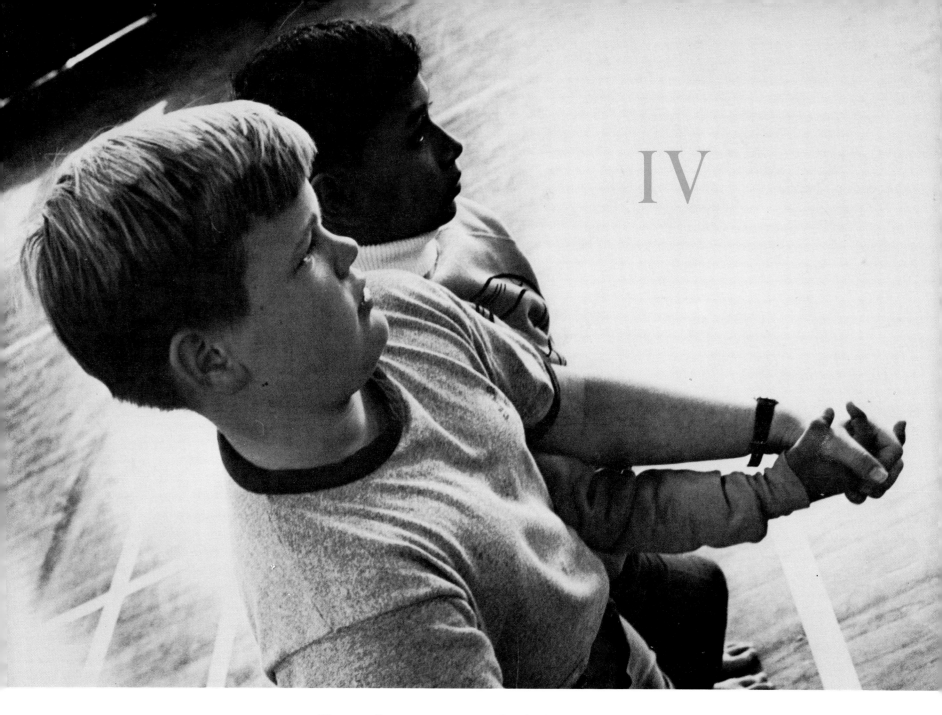

IV

Involve your children in Group Experiences.

Moving with others is a child's way of learning to trust others

STARTING POSITION:*

Use an eight-foot pole that accommodates six students side by side. Teacher and assistant each hold an end of the pole. It is held horizontally, about chest height. Move the pole in a slow, swaying motion from side to side. The students begin with their feet slightly apart,

EXPLANATION OF MOVEMENT:

"Rest your hands very gently on the pole. Close your eyes and sway with the movement of the pole. . . . As you shift your weight from one side to the other, bend each knee in turn. . . .

"Take off the hand that is nearest to me, and put it on your neighbor's shoulder . . . Keep swaying with the movement of the pole . . .

"Now take off your other hand and leave it down at your side . . . Without looking you can feel yourself moving with the entire group."

HINT:

Be sure the entire group is moving in unison before giving instruction to remove the hands from the pole.

DEVELOPMENT:

Start again with the previous exercise. When the group is no longer touching the pole, put it aside.

Ask another group of six students to stand behind the first group and, with eyes open, pick up the sway—both lines are going in the same direction.

Add another and another group until the whole class is involved. Try this both ways; holding, and not holding, hands.

HINT:

Try this to get a group to sing together.

ACCOMPANIMENT:
Silence is best.

Use of the pole was suggested by kindergarten teacher, Frances Scott.

SWAYING WITH A POLE

SIDE-SIDE BALANCE

STARTING POSITION:

"Everybody get a partner and stand side by side. Face front. Touch shoulders and hips. Hold inside hands, but reach them forward so that they're not caught between you. Relax your fingers."

DEMONSTRATION:

"Let's have Doug and Pepe demonstrate. Doug, lean against Pepe. Pepe, slide your outside foot to the side, bending your outside knee (like a small lunge) . . . But move slowly . . . and only when you feel Doug's hips and shoulders leaning against you . . . Both of you keep your shoulders facing directly front.

"Now it's Pepe's turn to be held. He gradually straightens up, shifting his weight so that now he is leaning on Doug. Move slowly . . . it isn't easy. You have to be very sensitive to your partner to find the balance. But it feels wonderful when you get it!"

HINT:

Keeping your backs up straight is the key to finding your balance.

ACCOMPANIMENT:

None. Silence is best for complete concentration on your partner.

DEVELOPMENT A: "SLANT BOARD"

"Let's do a different kind of balance. Stand back to back. This time Doug will hold Pepe's weight. Pepe, rest your hips and shoulders on Doug. Doug, as you feel Pepe leaning on you, slide one leg forward . . . into a small lunge . . . Keep your back straight . . . If your back is straight, then Pepe's body will be one straight diagonal line from his heels to his head. He will look like he is resting on a slant board."

ACCOMPANIMENT:

None. The concentration should be on each other.

To be in touch
TOUCH

DEVELOPMENT B: "ELEVATORS"

"Let's have Toni and Angie demonstrate another balance. Girls, stand back to back.

"This time balance is achieved by both of you pressing against each other with your whole back. Keep pressing as you both inch your feet forward and away from each other. Keep your hips and shoulders touching . . . Now bend your knees and go down together, close to the floor . . . Work slowly . . . Keep pressing and start coming up again . . . Keep raising and lowering yourselves, maintaining the back pressure."

HINT:

"Once you find out how far your feet need to be from each other, keep them there throughout."

ACCOMPANIMENT:

None.

39

SENSITIVITY

JUMPS

As preparation for Sensitivity Jumps, have the students do the individual "Jumps" going down the room, (page 28). Students should recall the feeling of constantly bounding off the floor, before working with a partner.

EXPLANATION OF MOVEMENT:

"Now you are going to do *jumps* with a partner. Both of you are facing front. Jump as you did before, bounding constantly. Stay with your partner. After three or four jumps try to match your jump to his, so that both of you are going exactly together . . . Don't turn to look at him. *Feel* him jumping next to you."

ACCOMPANIMENT:

None. Students must feel each other's rhythm.

DEVELOPMENT:

When they have moved together well in pairs, try doing it in threes, and then in fours.

PURPOSE OF TECHNIQUE:

To develop the muscular control needed to relate to your partner.

SENSITIVITY

TURNS

PREPARATION:

Draw two imaginary, parallel lines for the class, going from one corner of the room to the other. They are about three feet apart. Have two students demonstrate by standing, each on a line, facing each other at one corner, arms wide and feet apart.

EXPLANATION OF MOVEMENT:

"Turn with your partner as though looking into a mirror, reflecting each other exactly . . . Face each other, standing on your own imaginary line . . . Look into each other's eyes. Now turn away from each other, stepping on your own line . . . Keep turning in the same direction . . . Facing each other . . . Turning away . . . Facing . . . Move smoothly . . . Look into each other's eyes."

HINT:

If they are doing it correctly, one student is turning to his right, the other to his left. Students should have practice in turning in both directions.

ACCOMPANIMENT:

None. Silence helps the students to concentrate on each other.

41

EVERYONE has rhythm. Keep it alive with

RHYTHMIC GAMES

We are all born with a sense of rhythm. The regular pulse of the heartbeat is the foundation of this sense of rhythm.

The child who seems to have "no rhythm," is suffering an interruption of this natural rhythmic flow because of tensions.

RHYTHMIC GAMES, in which the child can lose himself in

movement,

fun,

group involvement,

will help him to relax and to gradually free him from inhibiting tensions.

V Involve your children through GAMES

Playing games is a child's way of learning.

TO THE TEACHER:

The game is accomplished in a three-measure phrase.

First measure (teacher's voice in rhythm):

"Simon —	Says —	Do —	This"
1	2	3	4

Second measure (teacher claps in rhythm):

1	2	3	4

Third measure (class claps in rhythm):

1	2	3	4

Have the class do this until they accomplish it well.

DEVELOPMENT A:

Ask a student to come up front to take your place—

"Who would like to be Simon?"

Repeat the game with the student leader, using his name instead of Simon's.

"Peter — Says — Do — This"

DO-THIS

DEVELOPMENT B:

TEACHER TO LEADER:

"This time, instead of clapping the rhythm, move one part of your body. Choose any part. Head? Okay.

TEACHER TO CLASS:

"Instead of clapping we'll move our heads for four beats, repeating what Andy does when it's our turn."

HINT:

Other parts of the body can be used: hands, arms, elbows, hips, knees, rib-cage, fingers, mouth, eyes, etc.

ACCOMPANIMENT:

Hit the drumstick on the wooden part of the drum.
Hit the drumhead with the mallet.

> "Andy — says — do — this"
> (Teacher's voice in rhythm)

1	2	3	4		1	2	3	4
	(side of drum)					(drumhead)		

(Repeat total sequence four times)

Little successes (quickly achieved in "Simon Says"), are necessary stepping stones to building confidence.

45

MOVE
AND FREEZE

TEACHER TO STUDENTS:

"When the music plays, you move. Do anything you like, as long as you keep moving. When the music stops, you freeze. Hold as still as a statue— even hold your breath . . . your fingers . . . your toes . . . your head."

NOTE:

Holding the breath requires deep concentration and creates a total alertness of mind and body.

HINT:

If you say nothing at first about "interpreting the music"—rather, emphasize the "freezing"—the students will tend to be less self-conscious. By concentrating on the "freeze" they can experience instant success. The gratification the child feels in this success, readies him for the development which follows. The next development leads into the interpretation of the music.

FURTHER DEVELOPMENT ▶

FREEZE
AND MOVE

DEVELOPMENT—TEACHER TO STUDENTS:

"This time we'll do just the opposite. When I play the music you will stay frozen—listening and holding your breath. When I stop the music, you will move . . ."

"Now hold it. Stay frozen while I talk . . . I noticed that many of you moved just the way the music felt, even though it wasn't playing. When the music was strong, you moved strongly. When it was soft and quiet, you moved softly and quietly. That was because you were listening when you were frozen . . . You seemed to drink in the music . . . You looked as though the music were going into your body . . . And then, when you moved, it all came pouring out of you . . . Let's see if all of us can *drink in* and *pour out* the music."

ACCOMPANIMENT: Side III, Band 3

MUSIC TEACHERS:

This is also a good game for familiarizing the students with a particular piece of music where you want them to learn to recognize various parts; such as "Carnival of the Animals" by Saint-Saens. Through feeling the different parts differently, they become aware of the subtler musical qualities.

Don't be too surprised if your students decide that a composer did not accurately title his piece.

WHEN YOU MOVE TO MUSIC

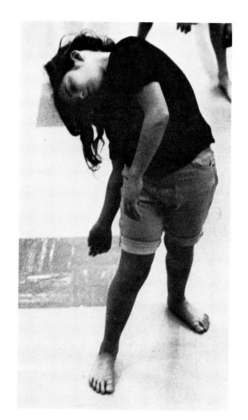

MUSIC WILL MOVE YOU

PREPARATION, TO THE TEACHER:

You clap on count 1. The class echoes your clap on count 2. The tempo is as slow as the *Giant Step* music (Side 10, Band 10), or you may think of it in these musical terms:

1	𝄽	2	𝄽
move	rest	move	rest
(you)		(class)	

Repeat this until the rhythm is clear. Give one or two students a turn to be leader.

1. CALL AND

GAME:

"Rob, you be the leader. This time on count [1], swing your body strongly into a position. Then hold still. The class moves on count [2], repeating the leader's position. Observe carefully. Hold still in that position while the leader moves again on the next [1]. On each count [1] Rob, you swing into a new position; on each count [2], the class repeats that position."

HINT:

Do not use the words "right" or "left" to designate direction. The cerebral process required for the student to identify the leader's right side and then his own right side, slows up and interferes with the spontaneous response. Instead, the instruction should be, "If Rob moves toward the window, you move toward the window."

Enrourage the timid students to be leaders.

ACCOMPANIMENT:
Handclaps or drumbeats.

FURTHER DEVELOPMENT ▶

DEVELOPMENT OF "CALL AND ECHO"

2. CALL AND OPPOSITION

Be sure that the class has accomplished the previous exercise well before going on to this development.

GAME:

"Until now you have been moving in the same direction as the leader. This time you will move in the direction *opposite* to that of the leader. Greg, you be leader . . . Greg will move on count [1], and you will move on count [2]. If Greg moves toward the door, you will move away from the door. If he goes up you will go down. If he moves forward you will move back. Don't worry about making your movement an exact opposite of his, just concentrate on opposing his direction."

ACCOMPANIMENT:

Same as *Call and Echo*.

HINTS:

Suggest to the leader that he make his movements large and strongly directional: *All* the way over to one side, or *all* the way up, or down, or forward, etc." This helps the group to see the position quickly and clearly.

There are many ways to interpret *opposite*. Encourage them to create individual interpretations: "Don't look around to see what your neighbor is doing. Find your own way of moving in *opposition*."

DEVELOPMENT:

In duets partners face each other and use the same rhythmic relationship established above. The leader swings into a position on count [1]. The partner swings into an opposite position on count [2].

52

*Praise sincerely but freely. Praise is a necessary ingredient to encourage
a child to further effort.*

FURTHER DEVELOPMENT ▸

FURTHER DEVELOPMENT OF "CALL AND ECHO"

3. CALL AND ECHO, IN CANON

"CALL AND ECHO," IN CANON

Be sure that the class has accomplished the previous exercise well before going on to this development.

EXPLANATION:

A canon is similar to a *round* in singing. The class mimics the leader's movement (same direction), always one beat after the leader:

```
L    L    L    L
     C    C    C    C
```

[L]—Leader, [C]—Class

HINTS:

Do not concern them with *lefts* or *rights*. If the leader moves toward the window, the class repeats his movement toward the window.

Suggest to the leader that his changes of direction be sharp and clearly defined, so that the class may more easily follow.

ACCOMPANIMENT:

Handclaps or drumbeats.

STATUES

PREPARATION:

"When I hit the drum, you reach upward as high as you can . . . Go! . . . While you are up there, think of different ways of reaching upward. You might lift one arm higher than the other . . . or turn your head . . . or twist your body a little . . . That's it . . . Now, on the next beat, reach downward in your own way . . . Good! . . . This time swing into a twisted position . . . Hold it . . . Stay frozen!"

GAME:

Encourage the students to swing freely to each beat of the drum, using extreme changes of direction. After five or six different positions, when the students least expect it, say, "Hold this position! You are now *statues!* You are frozen in the middle of some action . . . Think a moment and try to figure out what you might have been doing when you were stopped . . . Were you picking something up? Throwing something?"

Ask half the class to hold their positions, while the others try to guess the meaning of the *statues*. Encourage a variety of guesses for each position, so that the students recognize that each interpretation is a valid one. Try to pin down the guesses to specifics. When a student says, "He's picking something up." Ask him, "Does it seem to be heavy or light? Is it something precious?" The more the student tries to conceive the suggested reality, the more you are challenging his imagination.

ACCOMPANIMENT:

Single, sharp beats of the drum spaced by long pauses.

56

VI

Moving each part of his body is a child's way of learning about himself

PREPARATION:

"Stand with your feet apart. Imagine that you have glue on the bottom of your feet. They are stuck to the floor, but your body is loose and floppy like a rag doll. Your glued feet will keep you from falling."

For the very young: in pantomime, carry a pot of glue to each student and let him scoop out some glue to put on his feet.

EXPLANATION OF MOVEMENTS:
1. FULL BODY SWING

"Hold your arms out to one side . . . Your body is tall . . . Now drop your head, your arms, shoulders and back down between your knees . . . Now lift everything up to the other side. We'll go from one side to the other, dropping down each time . . . Drop — up — high, drop — up — high . . ."

2. UPPER TORSO, HEAD AND ARMS

"Now pretend that you have wooden legs and your knees can't bend. But everything else is still loose and floppy. We'll do the same drop and lift to the side that we did before, but the knees will be straight this time. Drop — up — high, drop — up — high . . ."

3. ARMS AND HEAD

"Now your whole body is wooden. Just your arms and head are made of rags. We'll do the same drop and lift, swinging the arms from side to side and dropping the head down to the chest . . . Drop your head each time and then look at the wall on the other side . . . Drop — lift — look, drop — lift — look . . ."

4. HEAD ONLY

"This time the arms are also wooden. Open them out wide to both sides. Only your head can swing from side to side. Start by looking out to the side . . . Drop — up — look, drop — lift — look . . ."

RAG DOLL

LATERALITY: *An awareness of both sides of the body is achieved through the constant repetition of the side-to-side swing.*

5. EYES ONLY

"Now the head is wooden. The neck is still. Only the eyes can move from side to side. Look down at the floor, then over to the side wall . . . Now down and up to the other side . . . Down — up — look, down — up — look."

HINTS:

On the body drop, the students should open their knees wide and bend the knees out over the little toes. This keeps the arches lifted.

Encourage the students to drop the head loosely from the back of the neck. This releases much tension.

"If you really drop your chin suddenly, from the back of your neck, you will feel a tingle down to your fingertips."

ACCOMPANIMENT: Side IV, Band 4

The music is a slow "three-rhythm" with a strong accent on the [1] for the *drop*.

PURPOSE OF TECHNIQUE:

To become aware of the feelings of relaxation and tension in the individual parts of the body.

61

MELTING

FANTASY:

"When I clap my hands, freeze into a snowman—a funny snowman . . . A carrot for a nose, a large, grinning mouth . . . a big, round belly . . . Hold a broom over your head, or out to one side—anyway you like . . . Everybody FREEZE! Hold it! You're frozen. You can't move!"

EXPLANATION:

"Hold it! You're frozen! The sun comes out . . . Your head melts . . . Your shoulders droop . . . Your arms drop . . . Your back drips . . . Your knees bend . . . Your whole body melts down . . . to a puddle on the ground."

ACCOMPANIMENT:

Your slow, gentle voice encouraging a gradual melting substitutes for music.

PURPOSE OF TECHNIQUE:

To become aware of the feelings of relaxation and tension in individual parts of the body.

SNOWMAN

The melting snowman image has a special value because there is a logical flow of body movement from top to bottom.

"READING" MOVEMENT

All teachers *read* movement. For example, when Billy comes into the room on Monday morning with his head on his chest, his feet dragging, you know something's wrong with Billy. He is one of the bounciest, noisiest boys in the class.

The way a child carries himself can give you insight into his attitudes, can provide a key for understanding sudden changes in learning attitudes.

Observe the standing and sitting positions of the children.

Observe them on the playground.

Daily practice in observation will make you skillful in *reading* movement.

VII

Involve your children through Dramatic Play

Play-acting is a child's way of learning about his world

PUSHING YOUR WAY

SCENE:

"You are pushing your way through water . . . Each part of your body is trying to make its way . . . Your legs . . . Your back . . . Your shoulders . . . head . . . arms . . . turn slo — ow — ly as you push . . . through . . ."

ACCOMPANIMENT:

When introducing the exercise, let your voice take on the slo — ow, hea — vy quality of this kind of slow-motion movement. As the students move, suggest that the "wa — ter is ve — ry hea — vy and ma — akes —you mo — ove ve — ry slo — ow — ly . . ."

THROUGH WATER

ADDITIONAL MOTIVATIONS:

"A shark passes by and you freeze in fear . . . And then you again move slowly, cautiously. . . .

You're trying to run, but the water holds you back and you can only mo — ove slo — ow — ly. . . .

You're trying to locate a friend, worried that his air might be giving out. . . .

You're searching for sunken treasure . . ."

NOTE:

Pushing Your Way Through Water is one example of a child relating his body to an environment. Suggest other environments for the students to explore, such as electric storm, sand storm on a desert, etc.

PURPOSE OF TECHNIQUE:

Awareness of equal tension throughout all parts of the body.

ROCKING CHAIRS

SCENE: (for young students)

"Let's be rocking chairs, rocking our babies to sleep. Get on both knees. What kind of baby would you like to put to sleep? I'm going to pass out some pretend babies . . . Would you like a kitten? . . . A baby bunny? . . . A real baby boy? . . . An elephant?"

EXPLANATION:

"Hold your baby in your arms and rock gently . . . Backward . . . And forward . . . Backward—not too far . . . And forward . . . Rock smoothly and hold your babies tenderly."

TO THE TEACHER:

Be sure that the children are not sitting on their heels. Each torso should make a straight, vertical line from the knees to the top of the head.

HINT:

The very young children like to use a real stuffed animal or doll. Suggest that they bring their favorite one from home. Be sure it is soft and unbreakable.

ACCOMPANIMENT: Side IV, Band 2

KNEE HINGES

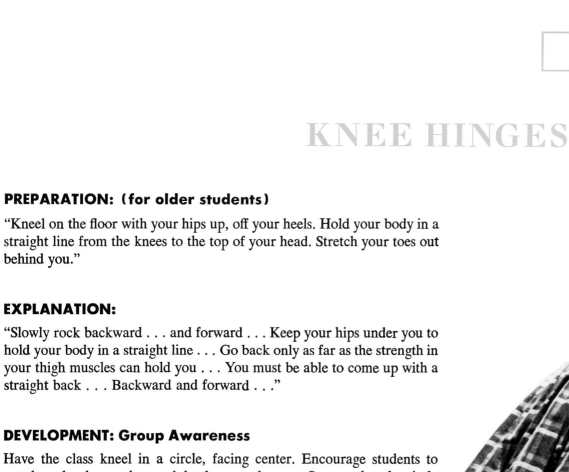

PREPARATION: (for older students)

"Kneel on the floor with your hips up, off your heels. Hold your body in a straight line from the knees to the top of your head. Stretch your toes out behind you."

EXPLANATION:

"Slowly rock backward . . . and forward . . . Keep your hips under you to hold your body in a straight line . . . Go back only as far as the strength in your thigh muscles can hold you . . . You must be able to come up with a straight back . . . Backward and forward . . ."

DEVELOPMENT: Group Awareness

Have the class kneel in a circle, facing center. Encourage students to watch each other as they rock back . . . and up . . . Suggest that the circle is one huge balloon, getting larger and smaller. This variation makes for group awareness and sensitivity and challenges those who are not rocking back far enough to "stay with the group."

ACCOMPANIMENT: Side IV, Band 2

PURPOSE OF TECHNIQUE:

To develop strength in hips, thighs and back muscles.

69

SCENE: (for very young students)

"You are a hungry kitten asking for milk. How do kittens ask for milk? . . . *Meow* . . . But nobody brings you the milk . . . So you ask again . . . *Meow* . . . But still nobody comes . . . You get very angry . . . What does a kitten do with his back when he gets angry?"

PREPARATION:

"Get on your hands and knees. Don't sit back on your heels. Keep your elbows straight."

EXPLANATION OF MOVEMENT:

"Round your back up toward the ceiling like an angry cat. Tuck your head under to push your back up higher. Push with your hands against the floor . . . Now reverse. Bring your head up, your back down, and say, *Meow*."

ACCOMPANIMENT: Side II, Band 2

SCENE: (for older students)

"You're an angry cat facing a strange dog." or

"You're a mountain lion at bay, surrounded by dogs and hunters." (Instead of *meow,* the older students *his-s-s*.)

CAT

DEVELOPMENT:

"On your knees with your feet stretched out behind you. Sit back on your heels. Your hands are on your thighs . . . Glare straight ahead at the dogs as you round your back in anger, tucking your hips under you. . . .

Now reverse. Lift your head, snap your back forward and *his-s-s*!"

PURPOSE OF TECHNIQUE:

To develop strength and flexibility of the back muscles.

EXERCISING THE EMOTIONS

We live in a culture where we do not express our feelings freely. Emotions MUST be exercised.

Just as we must consistently exercise our bodies for physical health, we must exercise our emotions for emotional health.

Dance class is the ideal place for emotional expression. The freedom to enjoy vigorous muscular activity exhilarates the child, and heightens all of his senses. Through movement he can be helped to exercise the full gamut of his emotions; to release strong aggression (*Swords*), and to experience peaceful inner awareness (*Swaying with the Pole, Mirror Reflections*).

He senses the wide range of emotions within him. He becomes aware of each emotion and how each one propels him.

VIII

Involve your children through their EMOTIONS

Expressing pent up feelings is a child's way of releasing tensions.

Sadness

Happy surprise

Shyness

Anger   *Joy*

An outward grace is an inner harmony.

HIDDEN ANGER

Anger is an emotion that is not acceptable in our culture
Children are taught early to *curb* its expression
Psychologists have made us aware that the repression of feelings can cause much harm to the personality and much tension within the body.

TENSION impedes the ability to learn.

In exercises such as *Swords,* we help the students release their intensely hostile feelings, harmlessly. Yet it does not lead to an uncontrolled situation in the classroom:

> *The structure of the story image*
> *The child's focus on using a specific part of the body*
> *Your reminder,* "Spread out so you don't touch anyone"

provides the *reality awareness,* so that full release can take place harmlessly within a structured framework.

The release of pent-up anger can:

> *Relax the atmosphere in the classroom*
> *Bring about an immediately improved ability to handle intellectual chal-*
> *   lenges more rationally*
> *Help to free the child of edginess at home and on the street.*

SWORDS

SCENE:

"You're living in the days when swords are the weapons used for fighting. You are surrounded by a hundred of the enemy. You must defend yourself. They're coming at you from all directions . . . You're desperate and angry . . . front . . . side . . . back . . . above . . . and below. You might be on horseback slashing at someone below, or you may have fallen off your horse and are slashing at someone above."

EXPLANATION OF MOVEMENTS:

1. ONE ARM

"Hold an imaginary sword in one hand. With large, slashing, angry movements, swing your whole arm in all directions (as if your arm is the sword). Don't focus on anyone in this room. Your enemy is in your imagination . . . Go!"

2. THE OTHER ARM

"This time the sword is in your other hand. Your stronger arm is wounded, so you are forced to use the weaker one. You must put out twice as much energy. Remember this is a matter of life and death . . . Go!"

3. HEAD

"Now your head is the sword. It slashes in all directions. Move from the neck . . . Go!"

4. LEGS

"Now your legs are the swords. Kick out all around you. Lie down on

78

your back. Slash with one . . . then the other . . . then both! Stand up and keep slashing . . . Lie down again . . . Change positions quickly."

5. BACK

"Now your back is the sword. Bend and slash forward, side, up and down. Thrust it front and back. Move your back in all directions."

6. WHOLE BODY

"And now with the whole body . . . Everything slashing at once!"

HINTS:

To avoid students using one another as "enemies" say, "Stand where you can move freely without hitting anyone. Your enemy is not a real person in this room, but a hundred imaginary men."

Keep the *head* section (number 3), very short, in order to avoid excessive dizziness.

It is difficult at first to locate the *back* muscles (number 5). In order to get the slashing action into the back, suggest to the students that they think of thrusting their diaphragms forward, as well as back.

ACCOMPANIMENT:

Strike the drum with the same desperate energy that you want the students to use. The rhythm is completely free and uneven—strong, sharp, erratic beats . . . on the drumhead . . . on the side of the drum. Use as fast a tempo as you can . . . Spurring the students to energetic action.

79

IF YOU WANT TO REACH A CHILD

BREAK THE   SPACE   BARRIER BETWEEN THE TWO OF YOU.

GET CLOSER TO HIM:

Partner him when the class is working in pairs.
Touch him sympathetically to correct a movement.
Look into his eyes.
Hold him when he gets dizzy from turning.
Join him in the circle.

Bend
    down
        for
            the
                very
                    small

IF YOU WANT TO R E A C H A CHILD,
R E A C H O U T TO HIM.

IX

Moving through space helps a child understand his physical relationships to his real world.

GROUP
CIRCLES

PREPARATION:

"Let's make a circle *without holding hands* . . . I'm standing in the middle
. . . As I turn . . . slow — ly . . . to face each of you, in turn . . . Adjust yourself to make the circle perfectly round . . . Good!

"What did you have to do to make a perfectly round circle?"

TO THE TEACHER:

Guide the students to such answers as, "We had to measure the space from
ourselves to you in the center." and, "We had to make the space on each
side of us even."

Encourage them to view the space at shoulder level rather than foot level,
so they can be aware also of the whole circle.

**1. "THE SHRINKING LAKE" (Smaller and larger circles)
STORY: (for young children)**

"Our circle is a lake. The sun is burning hot. It is slowly drying up the
water in our lake. As the water dries up, our lake gets smaller and smaller.
The edges of our lake come closer and closer together . . . Then the
clouds hide the sun. A storm comes up. The rain starts to fall. Water is
coming into our lake. Slowly it gets bigger and bigger . . . then it stops rain-
ing . . . and the sun comes out again."

EXPLANATION OF MOVEMENT: (for all age groups)

"Let's make the circle smaller . . . Take little shuffle steps toward the center . . . Keep the circle round, by keeping the spaces even on both sides of you . . . Move slowly and evenly with everyone else. When you feel your shoulders touching your neighbor on each side of you, stop . . . Now move out slowly again . . . Keep the spaces even . . . Move slowly with everyone else."

2. "THE BURSTING BALLOON"

"Let's stand in a small circle, shoulders touching . . . The circle is a balloon . . . I will stand in the center and pretend that I'm blowing you up (*blowing*) . . . You're getting bigger . . . and bigger . . . and BIGGER . . . When I clap my hands, the balloon bursts (*clap*) . . . Open your arms, turn round and round . . . fall to the floor . . . Get up again . . . Fall to the floor . . . On the next handclap come back and make another small balloon . . . I will blow you up again."

HINTS:

Give each child the feeling that he is needed by the group, "The circle will work only if *everyone* helps to create it."

Give students who need leadership experience a chance to take the center and blow up the balloon.

*"You can't make a circle all by yourself,
And we need you to make a good one."*

83

FURTHER DEVELOPMENTS ▶

GROUP

CIRCLES

(cont'd)

3. ROTATING CIRCLE

"Walk forward around in a circle, left shoulder to the center . . . Walk to the beat . . . As you walk center yourself in the space between the person in front of you and the person behind you . . . Watch the center of the circle . . . Walk eight steps forward. After the count of eight, walk eight steps backward . . . Then eight steps forward . . . and eight steps backward . . . Keep your spaces even . . . Now sixteen steps forward . . . and sixteen backward."

Also try "two," "four," and "thirty-two."

HINTS:

It's fun for the students to count aloud as a group.

Assure them that if they keep their heads turned toward the center they

84

will see the space in front and behind them, and still have a full view of the whole circle.

ACCOMPANIMENT: Side IV, Band 4

4. OPPOSING CIRCLES (Development of "rotating circle," Number 3)

"Form two circles, one inside the other . . . One circle faces with *left* shoulders to the center, the other with *right* shoulders to the center . . . As a result, when everyone walks forward, the circles are moving in opposite directions:

    a. Step in time to the beat, keeping your spaces even.
    b. When I tap you (or call your name) leave your circle and move to the other one . . . Everyone will have to adjust his spacing."

ACCOMPANIMENT: Side IV, Band 4

85

HUMAN SCULPTURE
(DESIGNING SPACE)

PREPARATION:

Before doing *Human Sculpture* review the *Call-and-Echo* exercises on page 50.

EXPLANATION OF MOVEMENT:

"I will demonstrate this with Jim. We will be using the same *one-two* rhythm you just used in *Call and Echo*. Jim, swing into a high position . . . Good, hold it . . . I'll take a low position because it's one good way of making a balanced design. (Illustrate a variety of design possibilities.) Notice that we are close . . . This gives us a better opportunity to design the space between us the way a sculptor does . . . We are two figures made

out of one piece of clay . . . The two figures belong to the same piece of sculpture."

SPONTANEITY:

Encourage the students to swing freely into a position—not thinking about it beforehand. If you notice too much control, return to the Preparation and Hints for the *Statues* exercise on page 56.

ACCOMPANIMENT:

Drumbeats, two alternating accents, one for each partner. Strike drumhead for the leader on count [1]. Strike side of the drum with stick for partner on count [2].

1. . .2. . .1. . .2. . .1. . .2

Children have an instinctive sense of design. If they can be encouraged to move freely and spontaneously, the layers of inhibition which covers this natural ability, will gradually be dropped. Give them time and many, many opportunities to break through the restrictions and release this natural sense of esthetics. Feel free to praise their small successes. Express your own enthusiasm. This will open the door to even greater spontaneity through greater confidence. Small successes give courage to try again. Each new try adds more fulfillment. The process is one of opening one door at a time, leading finally to a completely free expression.

GROUP

SCULPTURE

NOTE:

Be sure the students have experienced *Designing Space,* page 86, before attempting *Group Sculpture.*

PREPARATION:

Six students go to a corner of the room. They take numbers one to six. The rest of the class sit down front as audience.

SCENE:

"Here in the center of the room, an accident has taken place, a very serious accident. Think of how you feel about the accident."

EXPLANATION OF ACTION:

"First person comes running to look at the accident . . . He lands in a position that expresses how he feels . . . Then each one comes running, one at a time, according to his number, also taking a position that expresses his feelings. The position each take must be related sculpturally to those who are already there. By the time the sixth person has arrived we will have a group sculpture which we will call *Accident.* Remember to use a great variety of levels and directions."

ACCOMPANIMENT:

A short roll of the drum or a hand clap for each student's run, then an accented beat for the freezing into position.

HINT:

Take photos of the sculptures to give the class the fun of seeing what they've done.

MOBILE SCULPTURES

NOTE:

Be sure the students have experienced *Group Sculpture,* page 88, before going on to *Mobile Sculpture*.

PREPARATION:

Six students go to a corner of the room. They take numbers one to six. The rest of the class sit down front as audience.

EXPLANATION OF ACTION:

"Let's make a moving, mobile sculpture. Imagine that you're watching a circus this time. As you join the group, one at a time, you imitate the movement of something that interests or delights you. Relate the rhythm of your movement to the rhythm of the rest of the group, just as you relate your body position, sculpturally, to that of the total effect of the group."

OTHER MOTIVATIONS:

A rock band.

A group of girls looking out a glass door, watching a handsome boy walk by.

Each one of you is a moving part of machinery, fitting into the whole machine. (A boy's favorite)

Ask the students to dream up ideas for the rest of the class to guess.

ACCOMPANIMENT:

Rhythms are established by the group.

SUMMATION

The movement experiences suggested in this book can create a wholesome, enthusiastic vitality in the classroom, by making the individual child:

Self disciplined

More skilled in motor perception

More aware and proud of himself

More confident in bearing and posture

More accepting of the classroom challenges

Bumping and crowding in the classroom are minimized as children become increasingly spatially aware of their relationship to their environment.

These movement experiences can create a pleasant atmosphere in the classroom by harmlessly releasing fears and hidden angers, resulting in friendlier relations between student and student; and more open communications between student and teacher.

Dance, with its emphasis on TOTAL INVOLVEMENT promotes the harmony of the inner person with his own body, and the confidence to apply his TOTAL self to the space, the task, and the people around him.

GENERAL HINTS

OUTDOORS:

These movement suggestions work well outdoors if the class has the experience indoors first. They can then understand the framework and the goals when you take them outdoors.

FLOORS:

Wooden floors are best. If you have to use a cement or tile-on-cement floor, limit the number of jump-type exercises (jumps, leaps, gallops, skips) that you include in one lesson.

BARE FEET:

The children should work barefoot. It adds to their feeling of personal freedom and gives them a direct contact with the floor.

WARM-UPS:

Be sure to start the class with body warm-ups; such as *rag dolls* and *prehistoric animals.*

HOW TO INTEREST BOYS:

Use sport imagery; *swords, fencing,* etc.

Choose physically challenging techniques (*Elephant taking a shower,* jumps, leaps, *piano pushers,* sensitivity jumps).

Show the film, *Learning Through Movement,* for ages 9 and up.

VARIETY:

To achieve variety in spontaneous movement exploration, suggest:

> *Change your direction*
> *Vary your levels*
> *Use another part of your body*
> *Vary the amount of space you use*
> *Make your movements travel*

LIMITED SPACE:

When you have to limit the number of participants because of limited space, *involve* the rest of the class as an active audience; for example,

Have them do the rhythm accompaniment for the performers.

Ask them to solve a problem by means of their observation, such as: "Can you tell what Henry's statue means?"
"Watch and see if you can feel them *drinking* in the music."

In "Swaying With The Pole," organize the audience into sitting lines and have them sway in the same directions as the pole.

ALL AGES:

Material marked *all ages* is applicable to pre-schoolers.

Feel free to use material of younger and older age levels if it seems suitable for your class.

FIRST-LESSON PLANS

(Time: *approximately 30 minutes*)

These are suggested as first-lesson plans because they are simple enough for "instant success" and yet challenging enough to intrigue and motivate the students. They are well balanced because they represent different experiences in movement, and variety in the use of floor space.

All of the exercises in the book, marked for the age level of your class,

can be used as a "first-lesson plan." Be sure the class has had enough

experience with the original exercise before going on to "developments."

USING MOVEMENT IN OTHER CLASSROOM SUBJECTS

Appreciation of every subject can be amplified when children use their bodies to experience it. The following are a few of the ways that understanding can be increased through movement.

RHYTHMIC GAMES: MATH

A child can more quickly understand the concept of numbers if he experiences them with rhythmic responses of his body.

1. Have the children add and subtract with rhythmic beats of the drum. Start out with a number, "5" for example. Play it again, leaving out one. Then leave out two. Then three. Have the children accompany you with hand claps, head nods, etc.

2. Use Walks, Runs, Giants and Satellites, pages 10-14, to develop various mathematical concepts such as ½, ¼, double, quadruple, etc.

3. For E. H. and pre-schoolers—Indicate what page or chapter you want the children to turn to, by asking them to listen as you beat out the numbers on the drum.

4. Use the recorded music to accompany the recitation of multiplication tables, gradually introducing faster rhythms. Start with a slow rhythm such as Side I, Band 3; then Side I, Band 1; then Side I, Band 2.

RHYTHMIC GAMES: SPEECH

1. For drilling specific sounds, have the child repeat the sound to the beat of the drum. He stops when the drum stops, starts again when the drum starts.

2. At home, have the students write out ten boys' names that begin with "S." In class, going around the room one child says, rhythmically, "One name is Sam, what is another?" The next child must answer in time to the same rhythmic phrase.

RHYTHMIC GAMES: ART

"Imagine that you are deaf, that you cannot hear. Watch me play a rhythm on the drum without making a sound. Can you SEE the rhythm?" Have the students look for visual rhythms of movements. Have them transfer the rhythm to finger-painting, string-painting, etc. Suggest rhythmic variations.

RHYTHMIC GAMES: CURSIVE WRITING

"As you write, count the beats of the letters rhythmically."

ROCKING CHAIRS (KNEE HINGES): SCIENCE

Check for other hinges around the room. (See page 68)

HUMAN SCULPTURE: ART AND GEOMETRY

Observe for points and lines—where bodies cross you have points. (See page 86)

SPATIAL AWARENESS: MATH

Measure, using the body or parts of the body as a unit of length; i.e., "George's arm equals one desk length." (See pages 82-85)

SIMON SAYS: SOCIAL STUDIES

Play the game using a specific theme, such as "Airport," "Harbor," etc. "Simon Says Do This" (movements of a plane flying, the wind, waves, etc. See page 44)

SIMON SAYS: OTHER LANGUAGES

Spanish: "Simon dice haz esto."
French: "Simon dit fais ceci."

SIMON SAYS: SCIENCE

"Butterflies do this" "Alligators do this," etc.

STATUES: SOCIAL STUDIES

Suggest themes that you're studying currently for justifying the position, (after position has been struck), such as, "What could you be doing that refers to the life of Abe Lincoln?" (Answer: "I'm about to fall down after being shot." See page 56)

STATUES: ART

1. Model in clay one of the statue figures that you did today.

2. Using live models, "Draw the action lines."

STATUES: NEUROLOGICAL TRAINING

Have class observers guess, "Who is nearest to the window?", "The closest to the floor?", "The highest?" "The widest?". etc.

STATUES: LANGUAGE

Part of the class acts out (as statues) positions that describe:

A. Feelings—sad, angry, shy, etc.

B. Action—throwing, hammering, growing, etc.

The rest of the class, the observers, write or say what the statues are expressing.

STATUES: GEOMETRY

Observe statues and draw body in action, using geometric shapes.

STATUES: RELAXATION

Between tense activities (tests) use the *Preparation for statues* relieve tensions. (See page 56)

PARTNER BALANCES: MATH AND SCIENCE

1. Find other ways of balancing a partner. Relate to weights, levers and measurements.

2. Relate to principle of "forces" in back-to-back balances (elevators—See pages 37-39)

SLIDES: TRANSITIONS

Use *slides* and other traveling movements to get from one activity to another. (See page 29)

ANGRY CAT: RELAXATION

Do this at desk to relieve tensions. (See page 70)

PIANO PUSHERS: RELAXATION

To relieve tension at desks, push piano overhead. (See page 22)

MIRROR REFLECTIONS: SCIENCE

Whisper (secret) a theme to leaders for partners to mirror-reflect and guess, such as, "insect coming out of a cocoon." (See page 18)

MIRROR REFLECTIONS: MUSIC

For the purpose of recognizing theme changes in a specific piece of music, have the students change leaders whenever the theme changes.

MIRROR REFLECTIONS: PHYS. ED.

1. If a student is having difficulty coordinating in a specific skill (tennis stroke), have him partner a student who has mastered the skill.

2. To motivate a student to do additional push-ups, etc., have him mirror-reflect a competent student.

GROUP SCULPTURE: SOCIAL STUDIES

Use your own Social Studies themes for creating new group sculptures; such as forests for ecology, operating machinery, playground, etc. (See page 88)

GROUP SCULPTURE: ART

Take photo slides of group sculptures. Have class discuss and evaluate the compositional merits.

LEAPS: MATH

Measure the available space. How many leaps does it take to cross the room? How large is the room? How long is each leap? How high?, etc. (See page 30)